kawaii not
cute gone bad

i crap
rainbows

meghan murphy

HOW
BOOKS

Cincinnati, Ohio
www.howdesign.com

For more fine books from F+W Publications, visit www.
fwpublications.com.

12 11 10 09 08   5 4 3 2

Distributed in Canada by Fraser Direct, 100 Armstrong Av-
enue, Georgetown, Ontario, Canada L7G 5S4, Tel: (905)
877-4411. Distributed in the U.K. and Europe by David &
Charles, Brunel House, Newton Abbot, Devon, TQ12 4PU,
England. Tel: (+44) 1626 323200, Fax: (+44) 1626 323319, E-
mail: postmaster@davidandcharles.co.uk. Distributed in
Australia by Capricorn Link, P.O. Box 704, Windsor, NSW 2756
Australia, Tel: (02) 4577-3555.

Library of Congress Cataloging-in-Publication Data

Murphy, Meghan.
  [Kawaii not. Selections]
  Kawaii not : cute gone bad / Meghan Murphy.
    p. cm.
  Selections from the webcomic Kawaii not.
  ISBN 978-1-60061-076-9 (pbk. : alk. paper)
  1. Comic books, strips, etc. I. Title. II. Title: Cute gone bad.
PN6728.K39M87 2008
741.5'6973--dc22
                                        2007046358

Edited by Amy Schell
Designed by Grace Ring
Production coordinated by Greg Nock

ABOUT THE
Author

Meghan came rather late to her appreciation of all things kawaii, which may explain her strange reaction to—and her sometime misunderstanding of—the cute. Perhaps adorability was too rich for her blood, but it seems to have caused an odd reaction that produced the disturbing insanity (entertaining though it may be) documented in this very book, and online at www.kawaiinot.com. She is being well looked after, though the chances for a full recovery are slim at best.

Occasionally she draws things other than talking farts. These can be found at www.murphypop.com

Don't weep for her... she knew what she was getting into when she started this.

Gotta Give Thanks To

(OR I'LL BE IN TROUBLE):

Thanks to my mom and dad, of course. And my siblings Sean, Erin and Tim (who inspired and co-wrote the headcheese strip. How do you inspire a comic about headcheese, you ask? You probably would sleep better at night not knowing). And extra juicy thanks to everybody online who read, commented on, passed along, and in any other way dug the craziness that is *Kawaii Not*. I'd say you all have exquisite taste... but you already knew that, didn't you?

Introduction

What in the hell is *Kawaii Not*?

Well, *kawaii* is the Japanese term for "cute." As in, "Look at the fuzzy kitten, he's so kawaii." And *not* is an English term that means "not."

So what did I do? I combined the two by riffing on the sweet and simple style of certain Asian character designs, and made a wonderfully bizarre mess of it.

I started *Kawaii Not* as personal dare—just to see if I could produce something on a weekly basis. Why the four panels? Why the smiley faces? Why the blue background? I really have no answer except, "Seemed like a good idea at the time." Which I guess is the main *Kawaii Not* creative philosophy—along with, "Is this weird enough?" and "I'm going straight to hell for this one."

Cute Gone Bad. That's what it's all about.

Kawaii-lly Yours,
Meghan Murphy

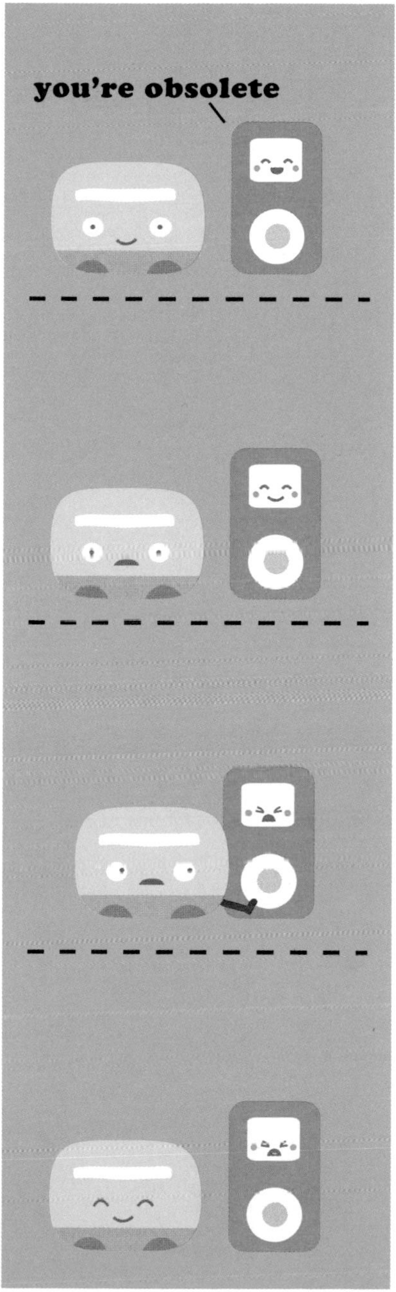
you're obsolete

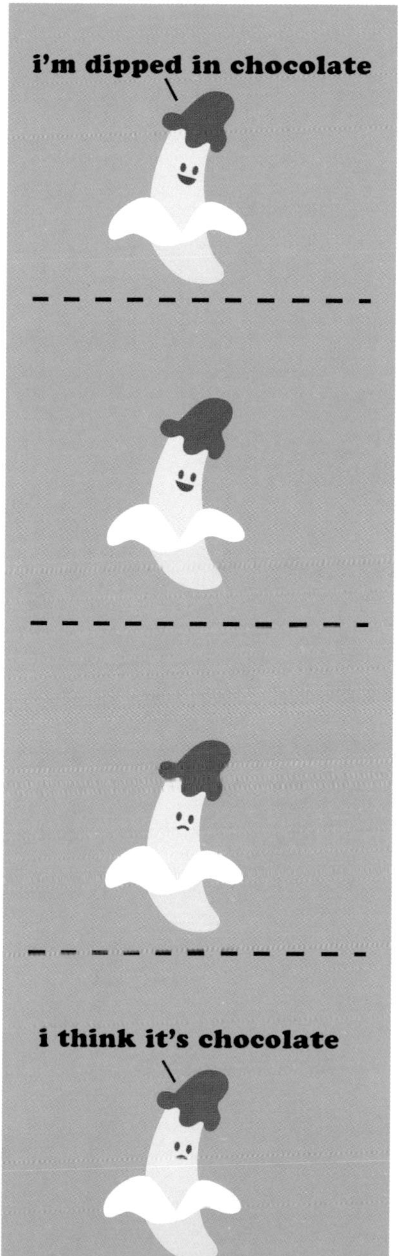
i'm dipped in chocolate
i think it's chocolate

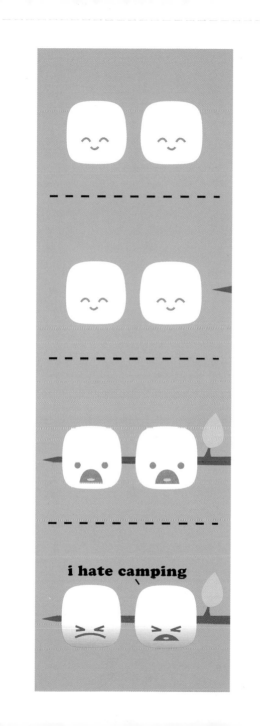

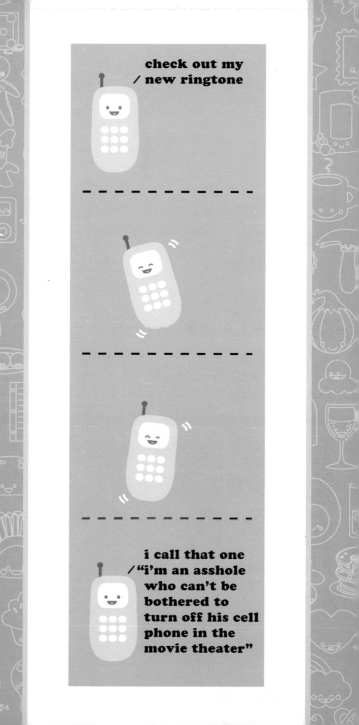

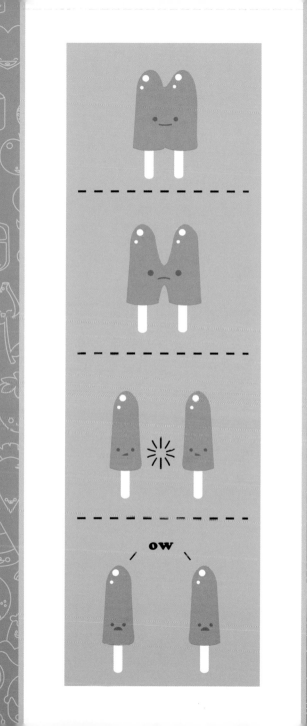

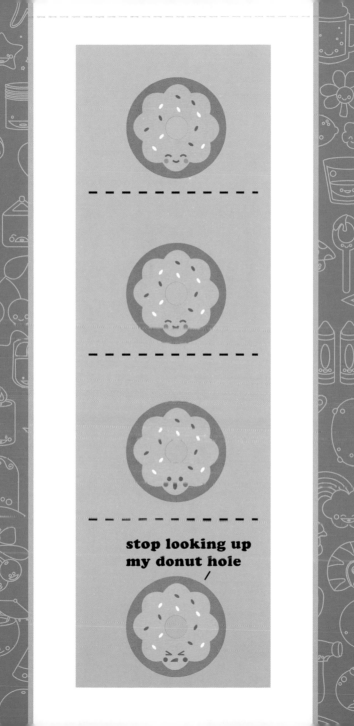

**stop looking up
my donut hole**

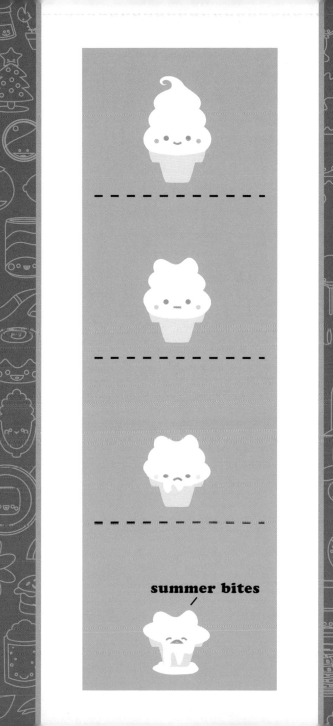

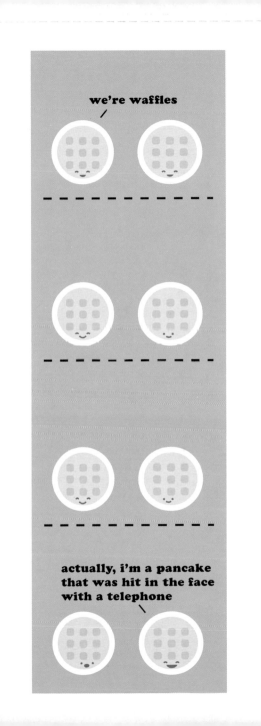

the birth of a fart

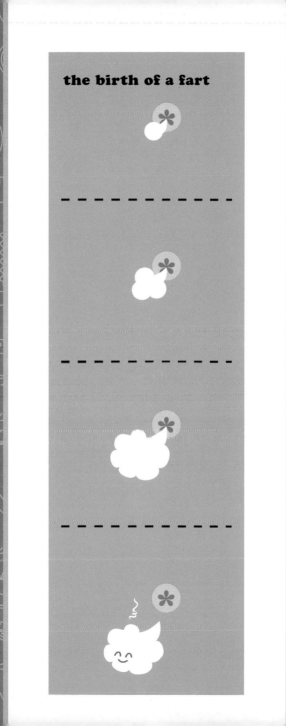

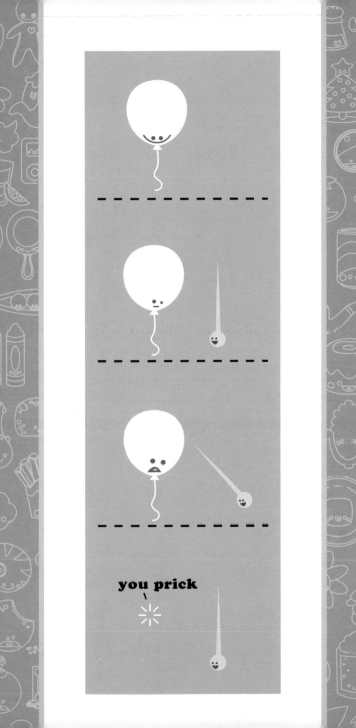

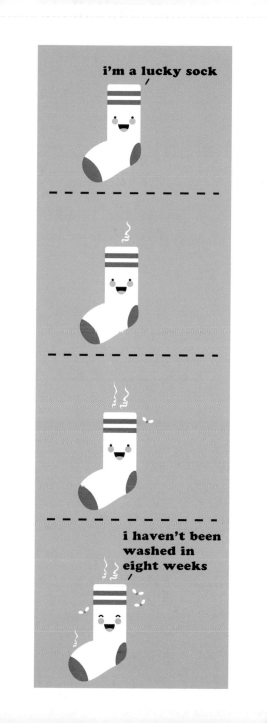

lick me

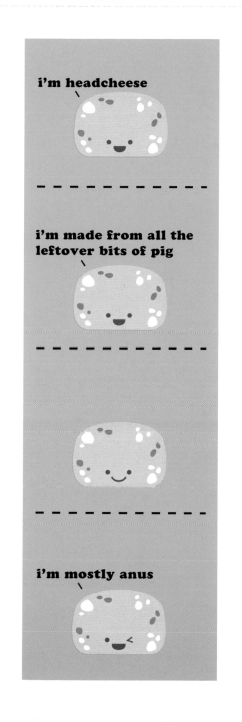

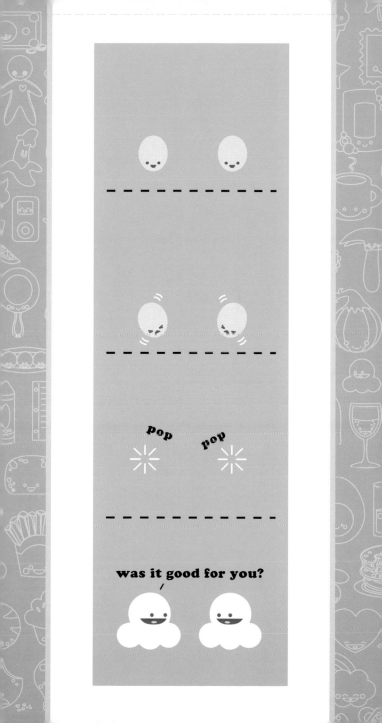

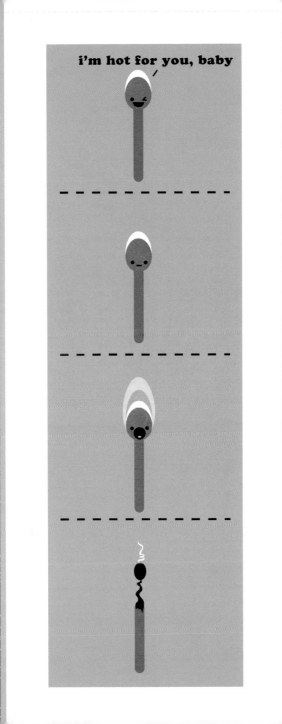

THE KAWAII NOT
Manifesto

And so it is resolved, seeing that the ENEMY is all that is sad and gray and includes all those who are taking themselves a little bit too seriously (frankly speaking), we do anti-solemnly swear to devote ourselves mind and body (plus whatever other bits might be lying around at the time) to the KAWAII NOT REVOLUTION! Be cute, be crazy, be free!*

And it is agreed that among our resolutions are the following. We will:

1. Draw smiley faces on everyone and everything
2. Know the cute side of weird, and the weird side of cute
3. Embrace the round, the soft, and all that's a little off-kilter
4. Know that nonsense is the best sense
5. Celebrate that life is sweet 'n' sour
6. Believe that it's okay to revel in the lame— we can't be cool all the time
7. Understand that we're all mad here
8. Recognize and enjoy the big softie that lives inside
9. Never suffer ennui … but instead have cherries jubilee!
10. Surrender unto the Squeee!!!

By working together to freak people out (in the cutest way possible, mind you), we resolve to bring the KAWAII and the NOT to all people.

Who's going to speak up for those inanimate objects that can't speak for themselves? We are! I'm sure we see pretty clearly into their cold, black hearts.

Above all else, we shall believe that anything, any time, anywhere can be cute… sometimes you just have to work a little harder to see it.

So in the final estimation, we draw but one possible conclusion…

Cute and Crazy of the World, Unite! And Save the World from Itself!

* Because things can get too serious sometimes, and if you don't find something to laugh about, the pressure will just build and build until it blows your head clean off your body. Is that what you want? A spurting geyser of warm, red blood where your head used to be?

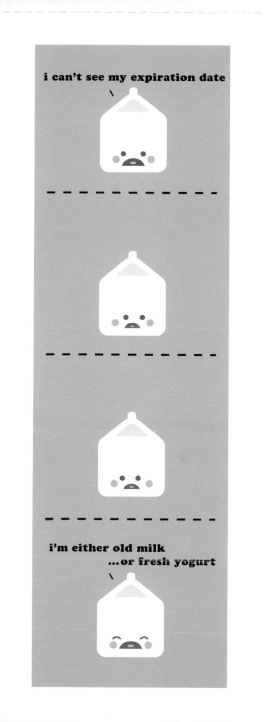

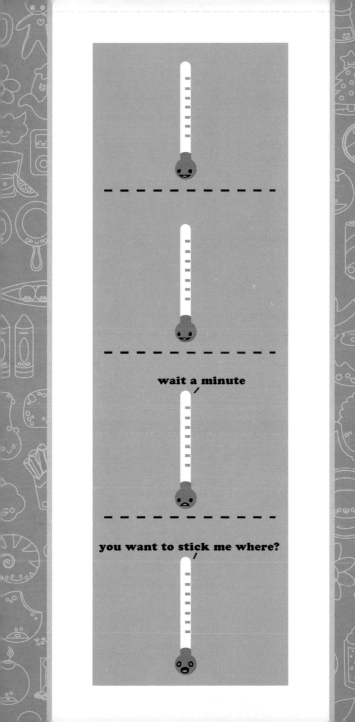

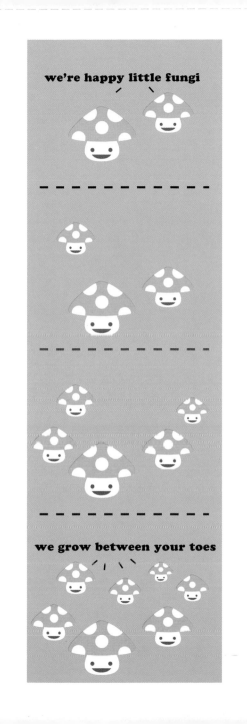

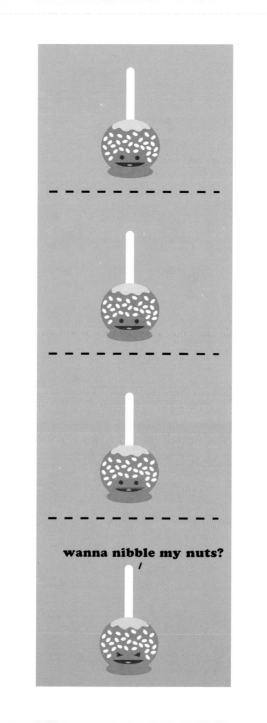

wanna nibble my nuts?

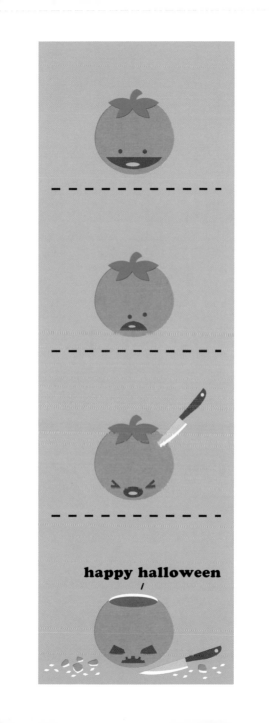

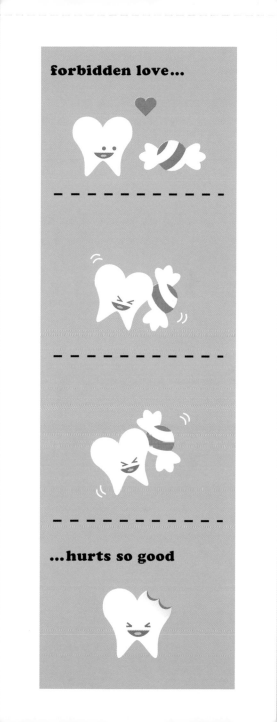

when i dream,
i bite your head off first

this tree is
shoved so
far up my ass
that my breath
is pine scented

you make me bubble

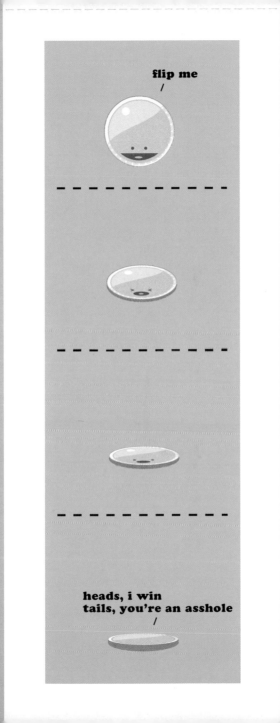

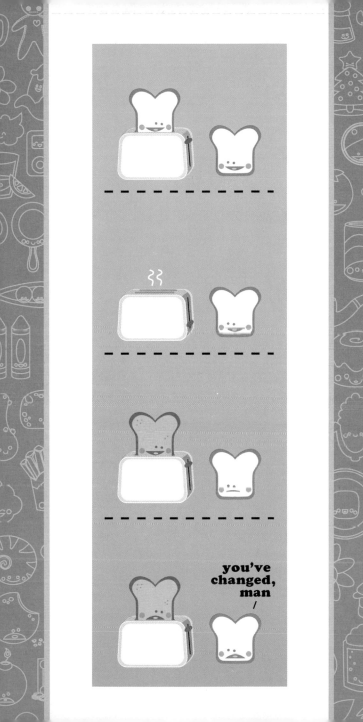

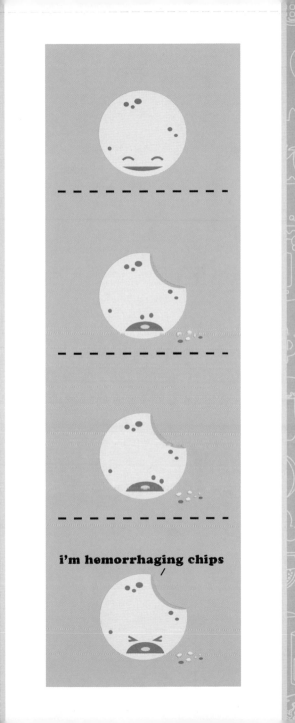

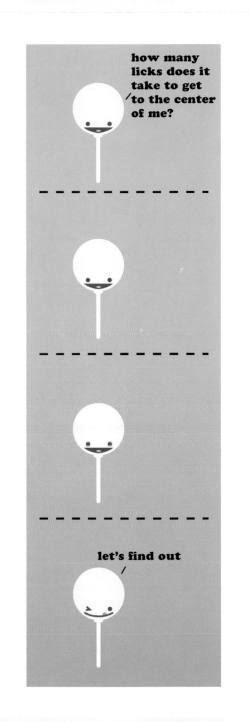

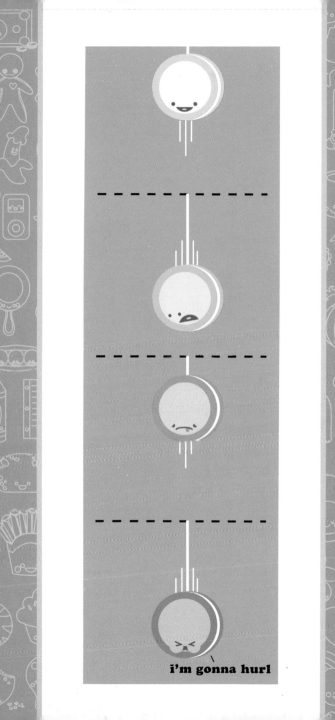

i'm gonna hurl

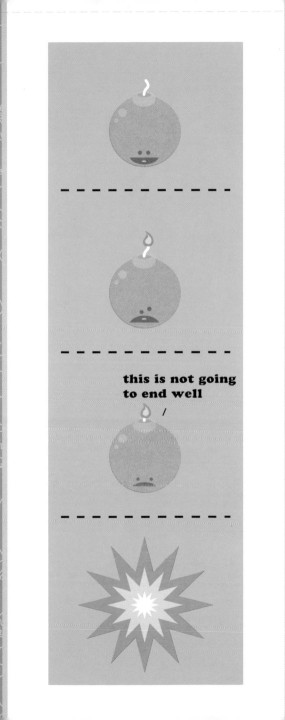

this is not going
to end well

Kawaii:

DO YOU HAVE IT?

We here at Kawaii Not Laboratories have dedicated considerable time and effort in our grand (yet adorable) pursuit of the essence of "cute." What is this elusive element? How can it be quantifiably measured? After decades of dogged (and surprisingly dangerous) research, we have finally created a simple—yet highly accurate—series of tests for measuring an individual's "kawaii level."

Section A: Physical Attributes

Approximate the size of your eyes. (Please try not to poke, puncture, or injure yourself in any other disgusting way while measuring.)

- **A.** They are about the size of a quarter
- **B.** They are about the size of an orange
- **C.** They threaten to engulf your outstretched hand (and are constantly sparkling)
- **D.** They are little black pinpricks of darkness

What description best fits your nose?

- **A.** It's in the middle of my face and has two nostrils
- **B.** It's the tiniest little nubbin of adorability
- **C.** What nose?
- **D.** With it I smell all the decay and decadence of this wicked world

Proportionally, how big is your head to the rest of your body?

- **A.** About 1/8
- **B.** About 1/4
- **C.** I am basically a head with little stubs for arms and legs
- **D.** Are you talking about my actual head, or my raging ego?

What emoticon best represents your actual appearance?

- **A.** :D
- **B.** ;D
- **C.** XD
- **D.** :P

Section B: Behavioral Observations

What is your giggle per day ratio?

- **A.** A couple giggles
- **B.** Continuous giggling
- **C.** I giggle, therefore I am
- **D.** What about my random bursts of weeping per day ratio?

You see a basket of kittens. What is your first reaction?

- **A.** To yell out, "Has anyone lost a basket of kittens? Anyone?"
- **B.** To murmer, "Aww...kittens!"
- **C.** To squeal, "SQUEEEEEE!!!!!!!!!!!!!!!!" (and fall over from cuteness overload)
- **D.** To assume it's some sort of trap

How much sugar do you put in your tea?

- **A.** 1–2 teaspoons
- **B.** 3–4 teaspoons
- **C.** I just keep scooping 'til the bowl's empty
- **D.** I only drink coffee that is as black as my soul and just as bitter

How do you normally show affection?

- **A.** With a hale and hearty handshake
- **B.** With a peck on the cheek
- **C.** *GLOMP*
- **D.** By dry humping

What is the one thing you can't leave the house without?

- **A.** Car keys
- **B.** Lip gloss
- **C.** A sunny disposition
- **D.** A nameless sense of dread

How do you typically end your e-mails or IMs?

- **A.** . (period)
- **B.** ! (exclamation mark)
- **C.** :D!!!!!!!!!!!!!!!!!!!!!!!!!!!!!!!!!!!!!!! (Either spastic excitement, or you passed out on your keyboard)
- **D.** I only communicate through ESP and smoke signals

Section C: Mental Attributes

A typical dream of yours involves ..

- **A.** Being naked in class
- **B.** Having a civilized tea party in an enchanted glade with forest creatures dressed in vests and spats
- **C.** Sliding down a rainbow into a marshmallow cloud
- **D.** The dark, eldritch elder gods stirring from their thousands-year slumber and reclaiming the Earth

What colors are the most appealing to you?

- **A.** Bold basics (red, blue, yellow)
- **B.** Pastels (baby blue, pink)
- **C.** Rainbow sparkles!
- **D.** Black

What is your biggest fear?

- **A.** Big, hairy spiders
- **B.** Failure
- **C.** Accidentally wearing unmatched socks
- **D.** Global thermal nuclear annihilation

How does your anger generally manifest itself?

- **A.** I slam my bedroom door
- **B.** I throw stuff around dramatically
- **C.** My bottom lip quivers oh-so-subtly, and I stomp my little feet
- **D.** I use massive amounts of profanity—I make nuns faint, and flowers turn to dust

What was your favorite toy when you were a kid?

- **A.** A cardboard box
- **B.** A teddy bear
- **C.** Pretty plastic ponies! And stuffed bears with symbols on their bellies! And fashion dolls with their own mansions and sports cars and boyfriends with no genitals!
- **D.** Creepy cymbal monkey—it told me to do things … bad things

Section D: Favorites

Accessory?

- **A.** Strawberry barrettes
- **B.** Cell phone charm
- **C.** Puppy in a purse
- **D.** Hip flask

Exclamation?

- **B.** YAY!
- **C.** NICE!
- **A.** SQUEE!
- **D.** SONOFABITCH!

Dessert?

- **A.** Fresh fruit
- **B.** Chocolate
- **C.** A fist full o' pixie sticks
- **D.** Insulin

Beverage?

- **A.** Earl grey tea
- **B.** Milk tea
- **C.** Bubble tea
- **D.** Straight shot of scotch

Smell?

- **A.** Freshly cut grass
- **B.** Freshly baked cookies
- **C.** Freshly spun super-sized, super-sticky cotton candy
- **D.** Freshly dug grave

Scoring the Test:

If you answered mostly A – Hmm, your kawaii levels are dangerously low. I prescribe a daily dose of rainbows, sunshine and cupcakes—the last of which should be injected right into your eyeball. Trust me.

If you answered mostly B – You have an average level of kawaii. You happy with that? Of course not! You need to take it to the next level of cute, my friend. Step up the adorable, pronto! We're counting on you.

If you answered mostly C – Oh my! You are the kawaii-est of the kawaii! Even big burly biker dudes melt into puddles of pink goo when you pass. Are you sure you're not some sort of furry baby animal?

If you answered mostly D – So … why the hell did you take this quiz in the first place, you cold-hearted bastard? Just get out, and take your baby seal club with you.

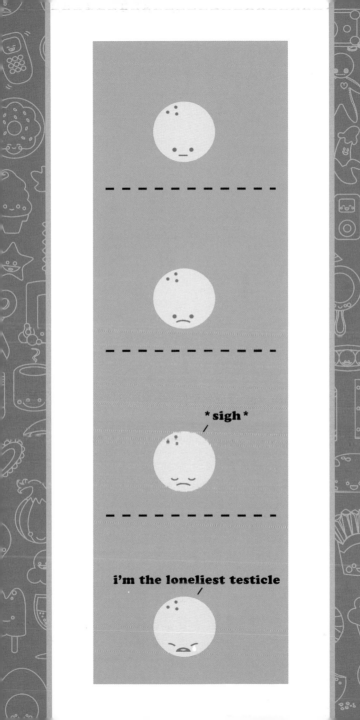

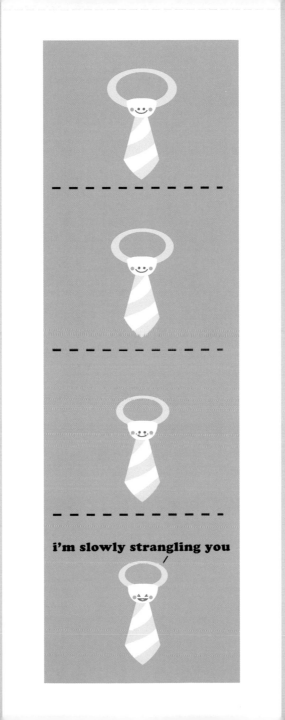

i'm slowly strangling you

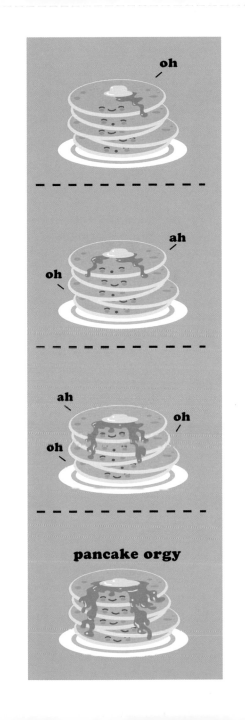

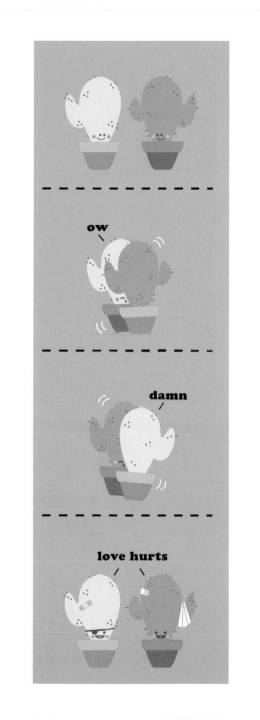

let's get shit-faced

i'm a BAD idea

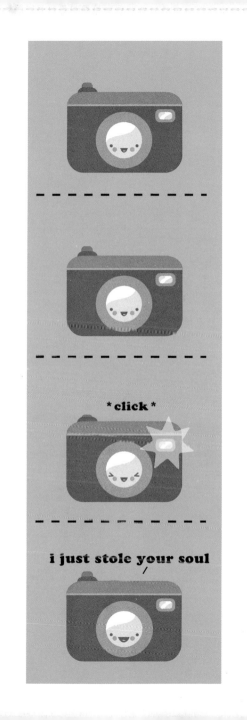

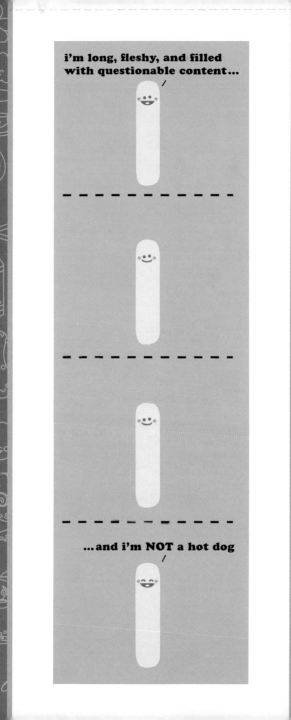

i'm burlesque

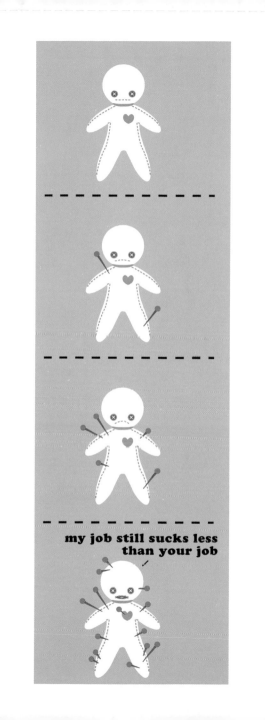

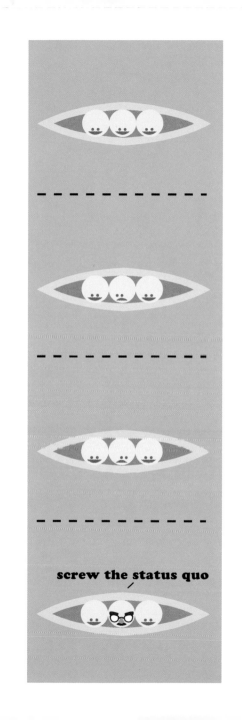

screw the status quo

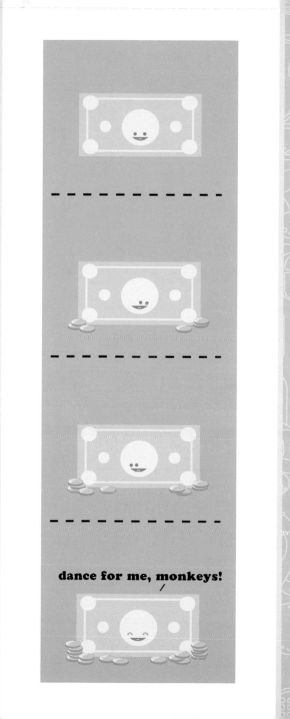

dance for me, monkeys!

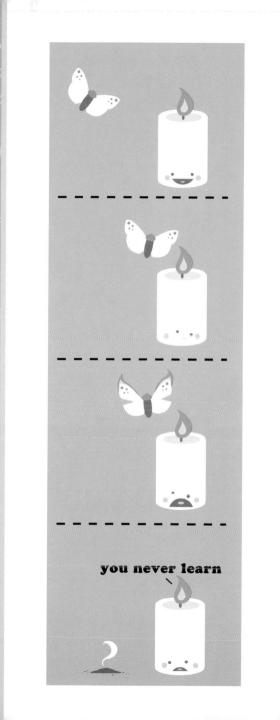

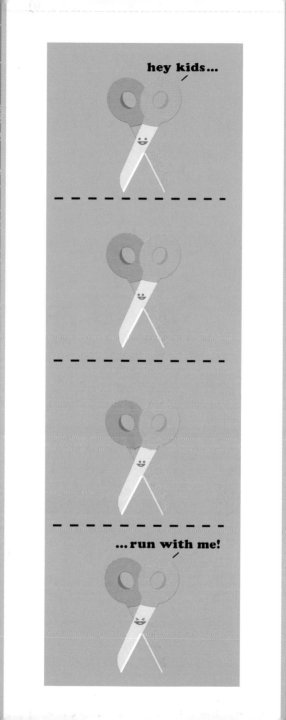

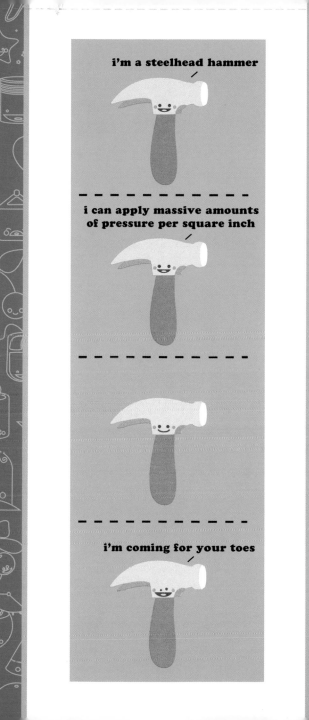

the moon is an asshole

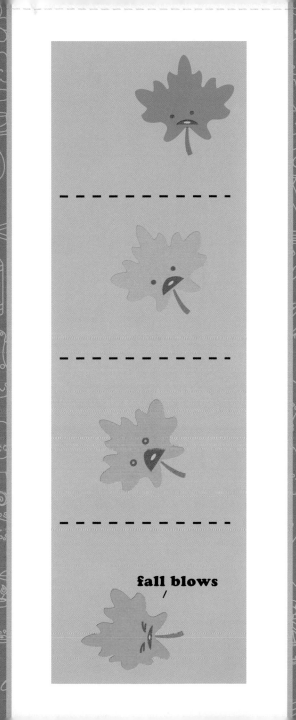

fall blows

THE BALLAD OF
the Cloud and the Fart

It happened many a year ago
On a bright and sunlit day
When two fine fellows came and met
Upon a well-traveled thoroughway

So alike these two gents seemed
As each looked upon the other
Like gazing into a mirror it was
And seeing a long lost brother

I am a Cloud, sir, said the first
As you can plainly see
I am so fluffy and so white
And as fresh as fresh can be.

And I can see, he did go on
We are quite the same
Perhaps we've met above before
Please tell me, sir, your name

The other looked a bit perplexed
And cocked one eyebrow high
Then a smile burst across his face
And glee twinkled in his eye

My gentle sir, he did begin,
We may be hard to tell apart
But if you lean in close you'll find
I am, in fact, a Fart.

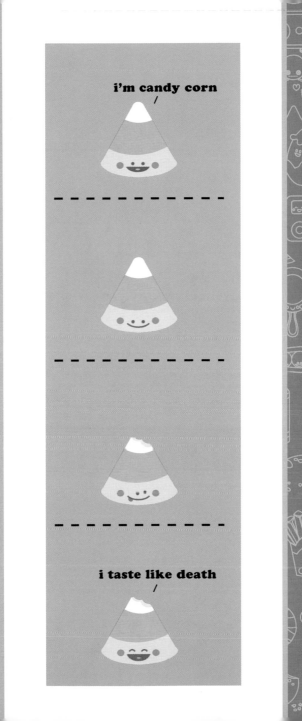

i think i have diabetes

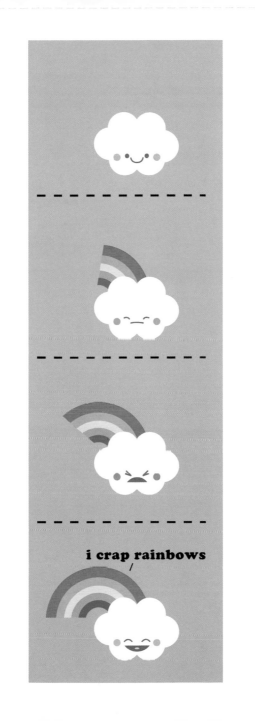

i'm a salmonella bomb

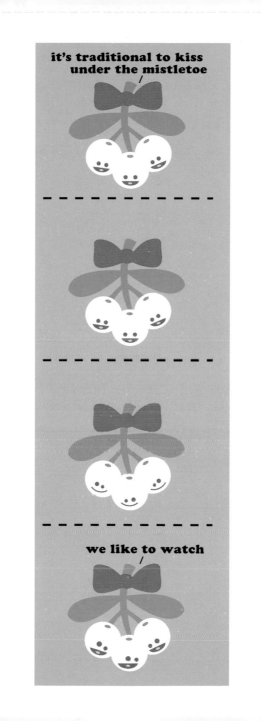

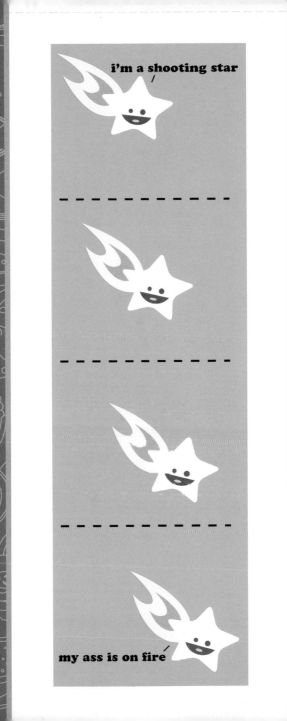

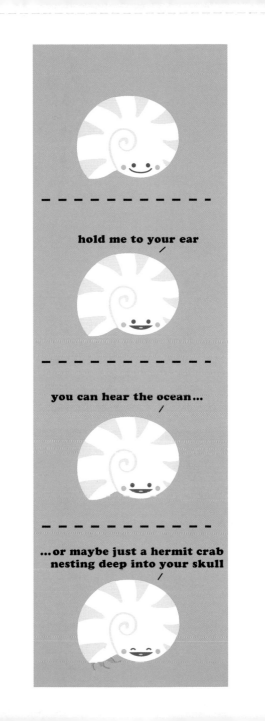

i'm raining on your parade

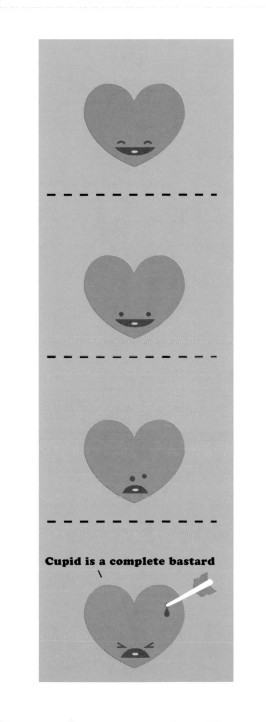

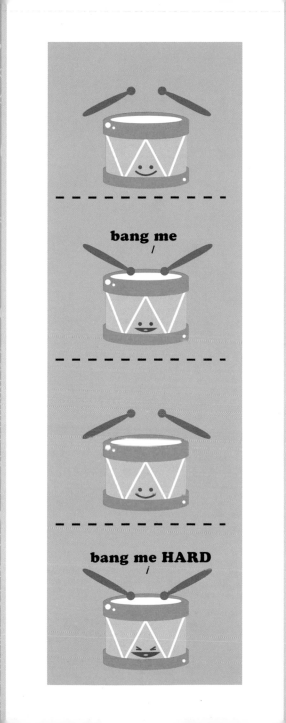

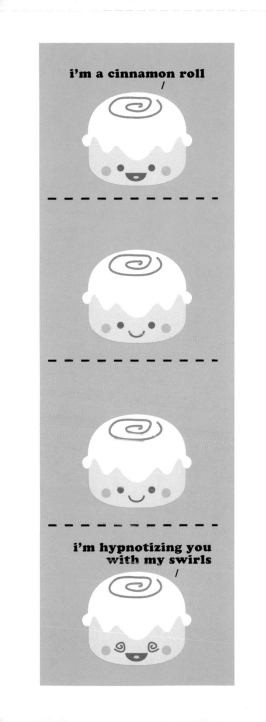

i hate spring

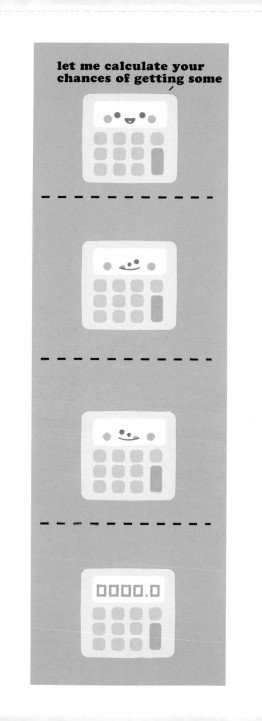

you are berry, berry lame

KAWAII-O-SCOPE

Croissant (March 21–April 19)

You are elegant and decadent. You are also kinda flaky. Your special color is buttery yellow.

Ramen (April 20–May 20)

You are cheap and easy—but I mean that as a compliment. Your special color is whatever's the most inexpensive.

Onigiri (May 21–June 21)

You are simple and direct, and you sure know how to accessorize. Your special color is seaweed green.

Tea (August 23–September 22)

You are an intrinsic part of many people's lives, but sometimes you take yourself a little too seriously. Try adding a little milk and sugar and give yourself a swirl. Your special color is perfectly brewed deep brown.

Creampuff (July 23–August 22)

Though you may appear fluffy and inconsequential on the outside, look deep within yourself and you will find—oh wait, more frivolous sweetness. Never mind. Your special color is cream (of course).

Strawberry (June 22–July 22)

Why you little tart! You are just impossibly irresistible (unless someone's allergic—then you are just deadly). Your special color is overripe red.

Marshmallow (September 23–October 22)

You can be squished, stretched, and even burnt on a stick—but you are always sweet and gooey on the inside. Your special color is toasted-to-the-point-of-almost-black.

Adzuki (October 23–November 21)

You are at your best when you are soaked, mashed, sweetened and crammed into things. Your special color is sugary red.

Pancake (November 22–December 21)

You are a fluffy, tasty delight—but naughty too. You are a dessert disguised as breakfast. Your special color is syrupy orange.

Spam (December 22–January 19)

You are full of mystery. And probably some snouts and hooves. Your special color is a very disturbing dark pink.

Miso (January 20–February 18)

You are a warm and savory bowl of comfort, but there are quite a few things bobbing up and down in your spiritual broth. Your special color is clear.

Mochi (February 19–March 20)

A sweet and sticky mess, often with a surprise nestled deep within. Your special color is whiter-than-white.

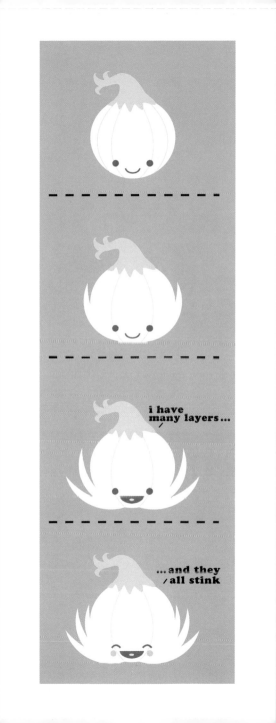

my niblets are showing

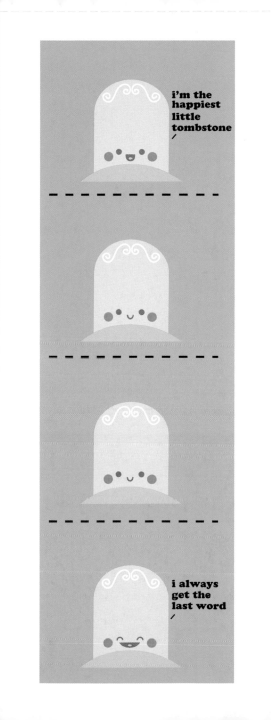

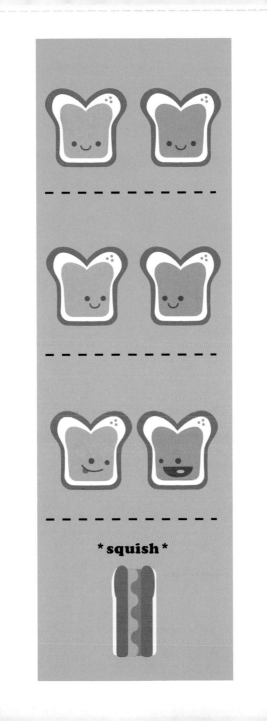

* squish *

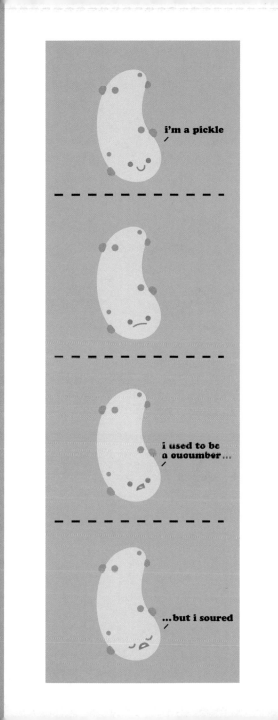

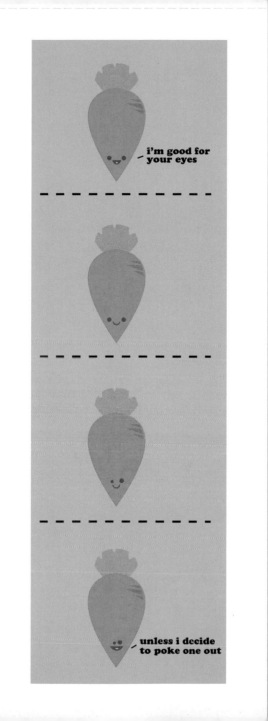

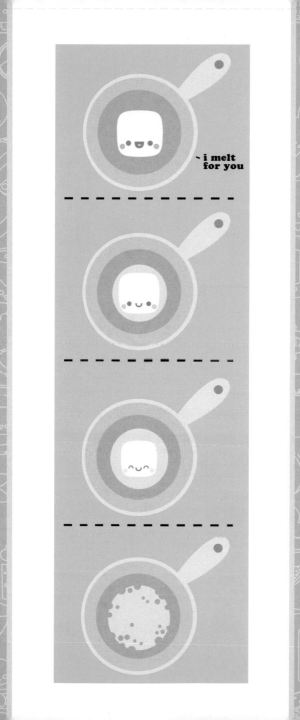

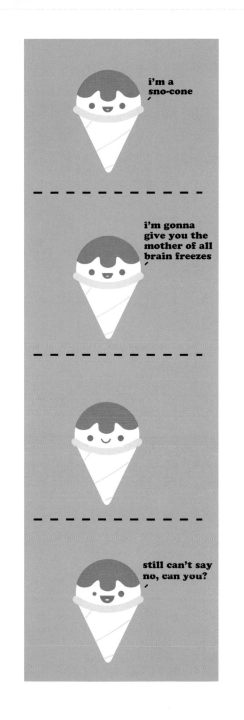

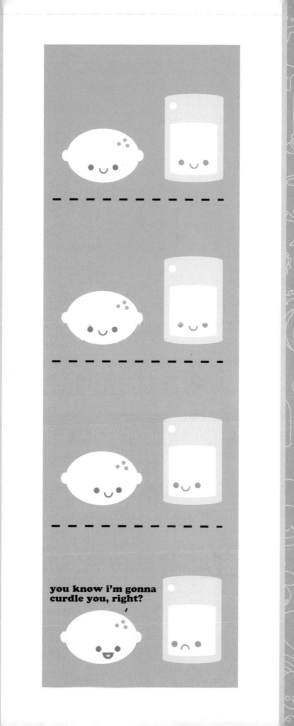

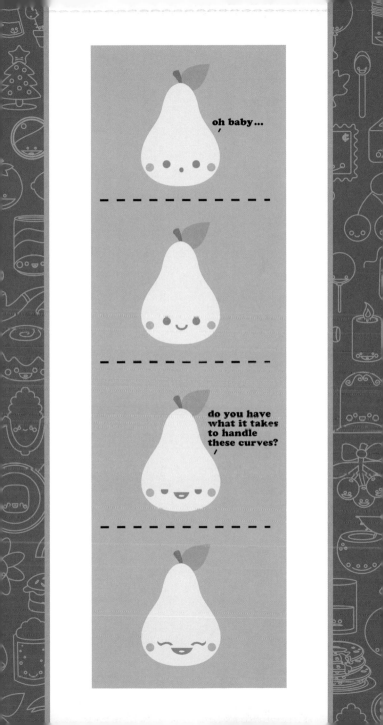

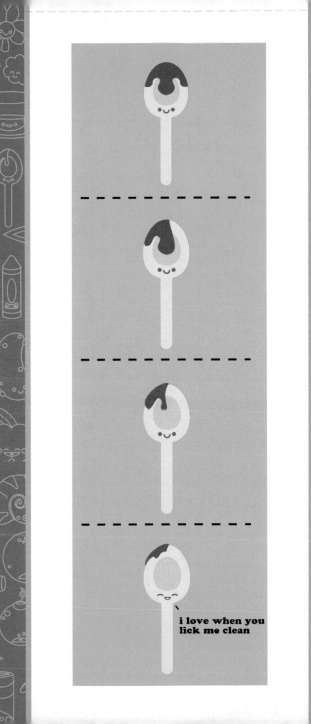

More Great Titles from HOW Books!

Milk Eggs Vodka
Grocery Lists Lost and Found
By Bill Keaggy

If we are what we eat, then *Milk Eggs Vodka* reveals deep truths about the average American with over 150 found grocery lists, including everything from the mundane to the marginally insane. The book also includes short essays on collecting, shopping, eating, and list making, and even some recipes that can be made from the ingredients on the list. Tasty.

ISBN 13: 978-1-58180-941-1, ISBN 1-58180-941-7, hardcover, 240 pages, #Z0675

Monster Spotter's Guide to North America
By Scott Francis with illustrations by Ben Patrick

From the mythical Sasquatch of the Pacific Northwest to the vicious Mexican goatsucker known as El Chupacabra, you'll read about the legends and major sightings of the most widely feared creatures reported to exist—plus a few you might never have heard of. Let *Monster Spotter's Guide to North America* be your guide and explore the legends for yourself.

ISBN 13: 978-1-58180-929-9, ISBN 1-58180-929-8, paperback, 256 pages, #Z0676

Dear Future Me

Hopes, Fears, Secrets, Resolutions
Edited by Matt Sly and Jay Patrikios,
creators of FutureMe.org

Delve into the lives of ordinary
people at their most honest. With
time capsule appeal, *Dear Future
Me* is a collection of letters written
by everyday people to their future
selves. This fascinating portrait of
real life offers a sometimes humor-
ous, sometimes poignant, but al-
ways insightful look into our culture and society—and
ultimately at ourselves.

ISBN 13: 978-1-58180-977-0, ISBN 1-58180-977-8, paperback, 256 pages, #Z0790

These and other great HOW Books titles are available
at your local bookstore or from online suppliers.

www.howdesign.com